FOOTBALL

RULES, EQUIPMENT AND KEY PLAYING TIPS

by Danielle S. Hammelef

Raintree is an imprint of Capstone Global Library Limited, a company incorporated in England and Wales having its registered office at 264 Banbury Road, Oxford, OX2 7DY – Registered company number: 6695582

www.raintree.co.uk
myorders@raintree.co.uk

Edited by Bradley Cole
Designed by Sarah Bennett and Katy LaVigne
Picture research by Eric Gohl
Production by Kathy McColley
Originated by Capstone Library Limited

ISBN 978-1-4747-4282-5 (hardback)
21 20 19 18 17
10 9 8 7 6 5 4 3 2 1

ISBN 978-1-4747-4284-9 (paperback)
22 21 20 19 18
10 9 8 7 6 5 4 3 2 1

British Library Cataloguing in Publication Data
A full catalogue record for this book is available from the British Library.

Acknowledgements
Alamy Stock Photo: GPI Stock, 20 (left), imac, 21 (right); Dreamstime: G0r3cki, cover; iStockphoto: strickke, 1, 17; Shutterstock: arx, 11, CosminIftode, 5, Dziurek, 19, liewluck, cover (background), 1 (background, middle), muzsy, 7, 20 (right), Pavel L Photo and Video, 9, v.schlichting, 21 (left), Ververidis Vasilis, 15; SuperStock: Blend Images, 13
Design Elements:
Shutterstock

We would like to thank Crissy Makela for her invaluable help in the preparation of this book.

Printed and bound in India

CONTENTS

Get in the game!

Imagine kicking a football into the net like Lionel Messi. Millions of people can't get enough of this action-packed game. What's better than watching football? Playing it. And you don't have to be a superstar like Lionel Messi or Cristiano Ronaldo. Start learning the basic rules and practise ball skills. Before you know it, you could be scoring your first goal.

"In football as in watchmaking, talent and elegance mean nothing without rigour and precision."

– *Lionel Messi, professional footballer*

FIFA WORLD CUP

The Fédération Internationale de Football Association (FIFA) World Cup is the world's greatest football tournament. Every four years countries compete to have the top football team in the world. Footballers play for their country instead of their club teams. A different country hosts the World Cup tournament each time.

LIONEL MESSI

FACT
Football is one of the oldest sports in the world. More than 2,000 years ago the Chinese played Tsu' Chu. In this game players kicked a leather ball into a goal.

5

CHAPTER 1

Ready to play!

Equipment

Footballers don't use much equipment. Their most important piece of equipment is a football. Official game balls weigh 397 to 454 grams (14 to 16 ounces). Football boots grip the pitch and make quick movements easier. Shin pads protect legs from kicks.

FACT

Goalkeepers wear padded gloves to protect their hands and help them grip the ball.

The pitch

Football is played on a rectangular grass pitch. A halfway line divides the pitch in two. The **referee** places the ball in the middle of the halfway line to start the match.

Goal lines run along the ends of the pitch. Touchlines run along both sides. These lines show out-of-bounds and in-play areas.

FACT

Most football pitches are between 90 to 120 metres (100 and 130 yards) long. They are 45 to 90 metres (50 to 100 yards) wide.

referee person who makes sure players follow the rules of a sport

Goal areas

A goal stands at each end of the pitch. A net reaches between two goalposts at the sides. The top of the goal is the crossbar. In front of the goal is a rectangular goal area. Goal kicks must be taken from inside the goal area. Around the goal area is a rectangular **penalty** area, including the penalty spot.

A FLOATING PITCH

Believe it or not, football can be played on water. Marina Bay, Singapore, is home to the world's largest floating football pitch. The float measures 120 by 83 metres (130 by 91 yards). Six posts tie the steel landing to the sea floor.

penalty punishment for a foul committed in the penalty area; if a penalty kick is awarded to a team, they are given a free shot on goal

CHAPTER 2

How the game works

Football positions

Each team has 11 players on the pitch. A goalkeeper guards the goal and makes saves. The other 10 players are forwards, midfielders or defenders. A popular team **formation** uses two forwards, four midfielders and four defenders.

As well as making saves, goalkeepers **clear** the ball far from the goal area. They watch the entire pitch and shout directions to their teammates.

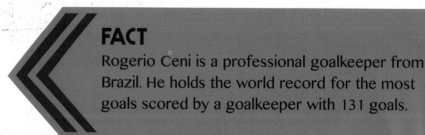

FACT

Rogerio Ceni is a professional goalkeeper from Brazil. He holds the world record for the most goals scored by a goalkeeper with 131 goals.

formation way the players in a team have been arranged to play
clear keep the ball far from the goal area by throwing or kicking it

Forwards are also called strikers. They spend most time in the **opponent's** half of the pitch and score the most goals. Midfielders switch between **attacking** and **defending**. Defenders are often the strongest players. They try to tackle the ball away from the other team.

FACT
Professional midfielders run up to 15.3 kilometres (9.5 miles) per match.

"Behind every kick of the ball there has to be thought."
–Dennis Bergkamp,
Former Netherlands footballer

opponent someone who competes against another in a game or contest
attacking trying to score
defending trying to stop the other team from scoring

CHAPTER 3

Rules of the game

Professional football matches have two 45-minute halves. A **kick-off** starts both halves. During the match, players try to score as many goals as they can. They also try to keep their opponents from getting the ball. Teams score goals by kicking or **heading** the ball into the goal. The team with the most goals at the end of the match wins.

"The only way to win is as a team."
–Pelé,
former Brazil international footballer, three-time World Cup winner

FACT
Football is played worldwide under the rules of the Football Association, which was formed in 1863.

kick-off kick that starts play
heading hitting the ball with your head

Referees and penalties

Referees call a **foul** if a player trips or pushes an opponent or handles the ball. When this happens the other team gets a **free kick**. Sometimes players are fouled inside the penalty area. Then they take a penalty kick from the penalty spot. The goalkeeper stays in the goal. All the other players wait outside the penalty area until the player kicks the shot.

FACT

Only goalkeepers can touch the ball with their hands. Referees call a handball foul when other players touch the ball with their hands.

foul action that is against the rules

free kick kick given to a team because the other team has committed a foul

Read more

50 Football Skills, Usborne (Usborne, 2014)

Football (Fantastic Sport Facts), Michael Hurley (Raintree, 2013)

How To... Football, DK (DK Children, 2011)

World Cup Heroes (World Cup Fever), Michael Hurley (Raintree, 2014)

Websites

www.dkfindout.com/uk/sports/football/
Learn more about this great sport!

www.motdmag.com/
Visit the website of BBC's Match of the Day Magazine.

www.theifab.com/
Visit the official website of the Football Association.

Index